6 Sigma
White Belt

Your Introduction to 6 Sigma

Contents

Define, Measure, Analyse, Improve, Control

Define, Measure, Analyse, Improve, Control

6 Sigma White Belt Course Outline

Course Objectives

1. Understand the basic principles and goals of Six Sigma.
2. Gain familiarity with the DMAIC process and its phases.
3. Learn about common Six Sigma tools, including process mapping and data collection.
4. Recognise the role of Six Sigma White Belts and their contribution to project teams.
5. Understand how Six Sigma can impact quality and efficiency in various processes.

Module 1: Introduction to Six Sigma

Topics Covered:

1. What is Six Sigma?

- Definition of Six Sigma as a data-driven methodology to eliminate defects and improve processes.
- Overview of Six Sigma's history and its application across industries.
2. Why Six Sigma Matters:

- Importance of reducing variation and improving quality.
- Benefits of Six Sigma for organisations, including cost savings, efficiency improvements, and customer satisfaction.
3. Six Sigma vs. Lean:

Define, Measure, Analyse, Improve, Control

- Brief comparison of Six Sigma and Lean, explaining how Six Sigma focuses on quality and defect reduction while Lean emphasizes waste elimination.

Activity:

- Group Discussion: Share examples of quality issues or inefficiencies in daily work, discussing how Six Sigma principles could address them.

Module 2: The DMAIC Methodology

Topics Covered:

1. Overview of DMAIC:

- Introduction to the Define, Measure, Analyse, Improve, and Control (DMAIC) phases.
- Explanation of how DMAIC is a systematic approach to solving problems and improving processes.
2. Purpose of Each Phase:

- Define: Identifying the problem and setting project goals.
- Measure: Collecting data to understand the current state of the process.
- Analyse: Identifying root causes of the problem.
- Improve: Developing and implementing solutions.
- Control: Maintaining the improvements over time.

Activity:

- Case Study: Review a simple, real-world example of a project that uses DMAIC to solve a problem, such as reducing customer wait times at a bank.

Define, Measure, Analyse, Improve, Control

Module 3: Key Six Sigma Concepts

Topics Covered:

1. Critical to Quality (CTQ):

- Definition of CTQ as a key concept in Six Sigma, representing attributes important to the customer.
- Examples of CTQs, such as delivery time, product quality, and service accuracy.
2. Defects and Variation:

- Explanation of what constitutes a defect in Six Sigma and how variation impacts quality.
- Importance of reducing variation to achieve consistent results.
3. Process Mapping:

- Introduction to process mapping as a tool to visualise and understand workflows.
- How process maps can identify inefficiencies and help in data collection.

Activity:

- Hands-On Exercise: Participants map a simple process they are familiar with, such as the steps in preparing a meal or handling a customer request.

Module 4: Basic Six Sigma Tools

Topics Covered:

Define, Measure, Analyse, Improve, Control

1. The 5 Whys:

o Introduction to this root cause analysis tool, where asking "Why" repeatedly uncovers underlying issues.
o Simple examples of how to use the 5 Whys in everyday situations.
2. Pareto Principle (80/20 Rule):

o Explanation of the Pareto Principle and how 80% of problems often result from 20% of causes.
o Application of Pareto charts in prioritising areas for improvement.
3. Check Sheets for Data Collection:

o Introduction to check sheets as a structured way to gather data.
o Examples of check sheets, such as tracking the number of customer complaints over a week.

Activity:

• Problem-Solving Exercise: Use the 5 Whys to identify potential root causes of a common issue, like delays in responding to emails.

Module 5: The Role of White Belts in Six Sigma

Topics Covered:

1. White Belt Responsibilities:

o Understanding the supportive role of White Belts in Six Sigma projects.

o   How White Belts contribute by collecting data, helping to identify problems, and implementing small improvements within their work area.

2. Communicating with Team Members:

o   Importance of communicating observations, data, and insights to Yellow, Green, and Black Belts.
o   Tips for effective communication and collaboration on Six Sigma teams.

3. Continuous Improvement Mindset:

o   Emphasis on adopting a mindset focused on ongoing improvement, even in small ways.
o   Encouragement to look for small changes they can make in their daily work to enhance quality or efficiency.

Activity:

• Team Exercise: Brainstorm areas in participants' own work environments where small changes could lead to improvements. Share ideas with the group.

Module 6: Introduction to Six Sigma Culture

Topics Covered:

1. Six Sigma as a Cultural Change:

o   Discussion on how Six Sigma can lead to a culture of quality improvement in the workplace.
o   Importance of employee involvement and commitment to Six Sigma principles.

2. Key Principles of Six Sigma Culture:

Define, Measure, Analyse, Improve, Control

- Customer focus, data-driven decision-making, and a focus on long-term improvement.
- Example of how White Belts can contribute to a supportive environment for Six Sigma initiatives.
3. Building Confidence in Six Sigma:

- Reassuring White Belts about the impact of their role in Six Sigma.
- Encouraging participants to be proactive in suggesting improvements and collecting data.

Activity:

- Reflection Exercise: Each participant writes down one improvement they can implement in their role. Discuss how they will measure its impact.

Module 7: Summary and Next Steps

Topics Covered:

1. Summary of Key Points:

- Review the main concepts covered in the course, including the DMAIC process, White Belt role, and key Six Sigma tools.
2. Applying White Belt Knowledge:

- How participants can apply what they've learnt immediately, even in small ways, to contribute to Six Sigma projects.
- Tips for staying engaged with Six Sigma, such as attending future training sessions or seeking mentorship from higher belts.
3. Pathways for Further Learning:

Define, Measure, Analyse, Improve, Control

o Overview of the next belt levels (Yellow, Green, Black, Master Black Belt) and what each entails.
o Encouragement to pursue Yellow Belt certification for those interested in taking on more significant roles in Six Sigma projects.

Activity:

- Goal Setting: Each participant sets a personal goal for applying Six Sigma in their daily work, including a timeline and measurable outcome.

Course Assessment

At the end of the course, participants complete a short assessment to review their understanding of Six Sigma fundamentals. This assessment might include:

- Multiple-choice questions on Six Sigma concepts.
- A simple case study where participants identify how they would apply a Six Sigma tool (e.g., 5 Whys or check sheets).
- Reflection questions to encourage participants to consider how they will use Six Sigma in their roles.

Certification and Completion

Upon successful completion of the course and assessment, participants receive a White Belt certification in Six Sigma. This certification signifies that they understand the foundational concepts of Six Sigma and can contribute effectively to process improvement efforts in their workplace.

Define, Measure, Analyse, Improve, Control

6 Sigma White Belt Course

Module 1: Introduction to Six Sigma (In-Depth)

---

1. What is Six Sigma?

Definition and Key Principles:

Six Sigma is a methodology aimed at improving processes by identifying and eliminating causes of defects and errors. Its goal is to enhance quality and consistency by focusing on data and measurable outcomes.

- Origin of Six Sigma: Six Sigma originated in the 1980s at Motorola as a way to reduce defects and improve product quality. Since then, it has been adopted across various industries like healthcare, finance, manufacturing, and service-based businesses.
- Six Sigma's Name: The term "Six Sigma" refers to the statistical goal of having only 3.4 defects per million opportunities (DPMO). This level of quality means that the process is highly controlled, with minimal variation from the desired outcome.

Understanding Defects and Variation:

- Defect: A defect is any instance where a product or service fails to meet customer expectations or specified requirements. For example, a defect in a car could be a faulty part, while a defect in customer service could be a miscommunication.
- Variation: Variation means inconsistency in a process. When there's high variation, the outcome is

Define, Measure, Analyse, Improve, Control

unpredictable. Six Sigma aims to control and reduce variation so that the process produces consistent results.

Example of Reducing Variation: Imagine a coffee shop where each cup of coffee should have a specific amount of milk. If some cups have more milk than others, customers get an inconsistent experience. Six Sigma would help find the reasons behind these inconsistencies (variation) and fix them to ensure each cup meets the standard.

Real-World Application: Many everyday companies, such as Starbucks or Amazon, use Six Sigma principles to ensure a consistent, high-quality experience. For Starbucks, this might mean ensuring each drink is made the same way each time. For Amazon, it could mean reducing errors in packing and delivering orders.

---

2. Why Six Sigma Matters
Key Benefits of Six Sigma:

1. Higher Quality: Six Sigma improves quality by finding and fixing problems that lead to errors or defects.
2. Improved Efficiency: By streamlining processes and removing unnecessary steps, Six Sigma makes operations faster and smoother.
3. Cost Savings: When errors and waste are reduced, companies save money on rework, recalls, and wasted materials.
4. Better Customer Satisfaction: Fewer errors, faster service, and consistent quality mean happier customers

Define, Measure, Analyse, Improve, Control

who are more likely to return and recommend the service or product.

How Six Sigma Creates Real-World Benefits:

- In Manufacturing: Six Sigma helps reduce product defects, improving product reliability and customer satisfaction.
- In Healthcare: Six Sigma reduces errors in medical records or patient care, enhancing patient safety and experience.
- In Retail: Six Sigma can streamline the checkout process, improve inventory management, and ensure that customers can find products quickly and easily.

Example:
Imagine an airline struggling with delayed flights due to inconsistent boarding procedures. Six Sigma can identify the causes of delays (like unclear boarding instructions or overbooking) and implement changes that speed up boarding and improve customer satisfaction. As delays decrease, the airline not only saves money but also builds a reputation for reliability.

---

3. Key Principles of Six Sigma
Data-Driven Decision Making:

- Six Sigma relies on data to identify problems, analyse their causes, and measure improvements. Decisions aren't based on assumptions or guesses; they're based on hard evidence.

Define, Measure, Analyse, Improve, Control

- Example of Data-Driven Improvements: If a restaurant finds that certain menu items cause delays during peak hours, it might use data on cooking times, order frequency, and customer wait times to understand and address the bottlenecks.

Customer Focus:

- Six Sigma projects are guided by what the customer values, often referred to as "Critical to Quality" (CTQ) elements. These CTQs help identify which aspects of a product or service are most important to the customer.
- Example of Customer Focus: In a bank, customers might value quick service and accuracy. A Six Sigma project in this setting would focus on reducing wait times and eliminating errors in customer transactions.

Continuous Improvement:

- Six Sigma is based on the belief that processes can always be improved. Even after a problem is solved, Six Sigma teams look for ways to make the process better, faster, and more efficient.
- Example of Continuous Improvement: A supermarket might start by improving inventory management, ensuring popular items are always in stock. Once this issue is solved, they might focus on improving checkout times or store layout to make shopping easier and faster for customers.

---

4. Six Sigma vs. Lean

While Six Sigma and Lean are often used together, they focus on slightly different goals.

Define, Measure, Analyse, Improve, Control

- Six Sigma: Focuses on reducing defects and ensuring consistency by using statistical tools to analyse and improve processes. Its strength lies in managing quality through precision and control.
- Lean: Focuses on eliminating waste and improving flow by removing unnecessary steps and reducing waiting times. Lean's goal is efficiency, aiming to create value for the customer with minimal wasted effort.

Example of Lean and Six Sigma Together (Lean Six Sigma): In a hospital, Lean might be used to remove non-value-adding steps in patient registration, reducing wait times. Meanwhile, Six Sigma could help ensure that medical records are accurate and complete. Together, Lean and Six Sigma create a process that is both efficient and high-quality.

Examples to Reinforce Key Concepts

Example 1: Coffee Shop Experience
Imagine a coffee shop struggling with customer complaints about order errors and long wait times.

- Six Sigma Approach: The shop uses data to find out when and why orders are being made incorrectly (such as misunderstandings at the counter) and identifies that certain steps in the process are slowing down preparation.
- Lean Approach: Lean principles would simplify the menu to make ordering faster and remove any unnecessary steps in the preparation process. Together,

they improve customer satisfaction by making orders more accurate and service faster.

Example 2: Grocery Store Checkout
A grocery store notices that customers are spending too much time in line at the checkout, leading to lost sales and complaints.

- Six Sigma: Using Six Sigma, the store could collect data on transaction times, identify causes for delays (like product code errors or payment issues), and create a solution to reduce errors.
- Lean: Lean would look at removing any unnecessary steps in the checkout process, like redundant loyalty program scans or excess packaging, to make the experience smoother.

Activity for Module 1: Group Discussion and Reflection

Objective: Help participants think of real-life scenarios where Six Sigma principles could make an impact.

Instructions:

1. Think-Pair-Share: Ask participants to think about a recent experience where they encountered inefficiency, delay, or error (e.g., waiting for a long time at a doctor's office, experiencing poor customer service at a retail store).

Define, Measure, Analyse, Improve, Control

2. Discuss: Have participants discuss with a partner or small group about how Six Sigma principles could help fix these issues.
3. Present Findings: Ask a few groups to share their examples with the whole class, reinforcing that Six Sigma principles are applicable to a wide range of situations.

Example Responses:

- Healthcare Setting: A participant might mention long wait times for appointments. Six Sigma could help by analysing appointment scheduling data to find and fix bottlenecks.
- Retail Setting: Another example could be finding expired products on store shelves. Six Sigma could identify why restocking errors happen and put controls in place to prevent expired items from being displayed.

Key Takeaways from Module 1

1. Six Sigma is a method for identifying and fixing problems in processes, focusing on consistency and quality.
2. The methodology is data-driven, meaning it relies on actual data to make decisions, ensuring that solutions are effective and measurable.
3. Six Sigma focuses on what the customer values most, meaning projects aim to improve customer satisfaction by reducing errors, variation, and waste.
4. Lean and Six Sigma work well together: Lean simplifies and speeds up processes, while Six Sigma ensures quality and consistency.

Define, Measure, Analyse, Improve, Control

6σ

Define, Measure, Analyse, Improve, Control

Module 2: The DMAIC Methodology

Course Objective for Module 2
By the end of this module, participants should understand the five phases of the DMAIC process and how each phase contributes to problem-solving and process improvement.

What is DMAIC?

Definition:
DMAIC stands for Define, Measure, Analyse, Improve, and Control. It's a structured approach to solving problems and making processes more efficient and consistent. Each phase of DMAIC has specific goals, tools, and methods that help guide a project from identifying a problem to ensuring lasting improvements.

Simple Analogy:
Imagine trying to improve how you prepare breakfast each morning. Using DMAIC, you'd start by identifying what you want to improve (Define), figuring out how long each step currently takes (Measure), understanding why certain steps are taking too long (Analyse), making changes to improve efficiency (Improve), and then keeping those changes in place to ensure breakfast is consistently faster in the future (Control).

Define, Measure, Analyse, Improve, Control

Phase 1: Define

Goal:
Clearly identify the problem, set specific goals, and understand the customer's needs.

Key Activities:

1. Identify the Problem: Define what needs to be improved. This could be a specific issue, like a product defect or long customer wait times.
2. Define Project Goals: Set clear, measurable goals. For example, "Reduce average customer wait time by 30%."
3. Determine the Scope: Define the boundaries of the project to keep it manageable.
4. Identify Stakeholders: Identify who is impacted by the problem and who will benefit from the solution.

Example:
Imagine a pizza restaurant experiencing customer complaints about long delivery times. In the Define phase, the team might set a goal to reduce delivery times by 20% to improve customer satisfaction. They'll specify which departments (kitchen, delivery) are involved and clarify which customers (local area) are affected.

Tools:

- Project Charter: A document that outlines the problem, goals, scope, and stakeholders.

Define, Measure, Analyse, Improve, Control

- SIPOC Diagram: A high-level map of the process showing Suppliers, Inputs, Process, Outputs, and Customers.

Phase 2: Measure

Goal:
Collect data to understand the current state of the process and establish a baseline. The goal is to quantify the problem and identify performance gaps.

Key Activities:

1. Identify Metrics: Select key metrics to measure performance (e.g., customer wait time, defect rate).
2. Collect Data: Gather accurate data related to the current process. This could involve timing steps, counting errors, or collecting customer feedback.
3. Establish a Baseline: Use the data to create a snapshot of the process's current performance. This baseline helps compare improvements later on.

Example:
In the pizza delivery example, the team might measure the current average delivery time, the time taken at each stage (order, cooking, packaging, delivery), and customer feedback about delivery speed.

Tools:

- Check Sheets: Simple forms used to collect data in a structured way.

- Process Mapping: Visual maps of the steps in the process to understand where time is spent or errors occur.

Phase 3: Analyse

Goal:
Identify the root causes of the problem by analysing the data and process. In this phase, the team seeks to understand **why** the problem is happening.

Key Activities:

1. Identify Root Causes: Use tools to dig deeper into potential causes of the problem, going beyond symptoms.
2. Analyse Data: Look for patterns, bottlenecks, and areas with high variation or errors.
3. Validate Root Causes: Ensure that the identified causes are actually contributing to the problem. This can be done through testing or further data analysis.

Example:
The pizza restaurant might find that the delivery delay is due to multiple issues, like prep delays, poor communication with delivery drivers, and mismanaged packaging. By validating these root causes, they confirm that addressing them would improve delivery times.

Tools:

- 5 Whys: A simple tool that asks "Why?" repeatedly to get to the root cause.
- Fishbone Diagram: A visual tool to brainstorm potential causes, often used to identify categories of issues (e.g., people, process, materials).
- Pareto Chart: Shows the most frequent causes or issues, helping teams focus on the biggest contributors.

Phase 4: Improve

Goal:
Develop and implement solutions to address the root causes identified in the Analyse phase. This phase is about making changes to improve the process.

Key Activities:

1. Brainstorm Solutions: Generate ideas to address the root causes.
2. Evaluate Solutions: Select the best solutions by considering feasibility, impact, and cost.
3. Implement Changes: Make the selected changes to the process, such as changing procedures, adding tools, or training staff.
4. Test Improvements: Pilot the changes to see if they achieve the desired results before fully rolling them out.

Example:
The pizza restaurant could decide to prepare certain ingredients ahead of time to reduce cooking delays, introduce a real-time delivery tracking system, and

Define, Measure, Analyse, Improve, Control

update packaging procedures to make it faster for drivers to collect orders.

Tools:

- Brainstorming: Group sessions to generate improvement ideas.
- Pilot Testing: Testing changes on a small scale before full implementation.
- Process Simulation: Simulating the process with changes to predict their impact.

Phase 5: Control

Goal:
Ensure that the improvements are sustained over time. This phase involves setting up monitoring systems to make sure the process stays on track.

Key Activities:

1. Develop Control Plans: Define how the process will be monitored, with clear performance standards.
2. Create Monitoring Systems: Set up dashboards or regular reports to track performance.
3. Standardise Changes: Document the improved process and create training materials if needed.
4. Address New Issues: Have a plan for addressing any issues that arise in the future.

Example:
The pizza restaurant might introduce a dashboard to

Define, Measure, Analyse, Improve, Control

monitor average delivery times and set a standard operating procedure for preparing orders. They could also implement regular training for kitchen staff and delivery drivers to maintain the improved process.

Tools:

- Control Charts: Track process performance over time to detect any deviations.
- Standard Operating Procedures (SOPs): Detailed instructions to ensure everyone follows the same process.
- Audits: Regular checks to verify that standards are maintained.

Example Walkthrough: Using DMAIC for Reducing Customer Wait Times in a Bank

To reinforce the DMAIC phases, here's a practical example of how each phase might look when applied to a real-world issue – reducing customer wait times in a bank.

1. Define: The bank identifies that wait times are too long, leading to customer complaints. They set a goal to reduce wait times by 20%.
2. Measure: The bank collects data on current wait times and finds that the average wait time is 15 minutes, with many customers waiting over 20 minutes during peak hours.
3. Analyse: They analyse the data and find that the main causes are insufficient staff during peak times,

Define, Measure, Analyse, Improve, Control

inefficient check-in procedures, and delays in the
queueing system.

4. Improve: The bank decides to streamline check-in,
adjust staffing levels during peak hours, and implement
a digital queue system where customers are called
based on the order of arrival.

5. Control: They set up a system to track wait times daily,
train staff on the new check-in procedures, and conduct
regular audits to ensure that wait times stay within the
target.

Activity for Module 2: Case Study Exercise

Objective: Reinforce understanding of each DMAIC
phase by applying it to a simple case study.

Case Study:

- A hospital wants to reduce the average time it takes to
discharge patients after a doctor signs off. Currently, the
process is taking longer than expected, leading to delays
and affecting patient satisfaction.

Instructions:

1. Divide participants into small groups and have each
group discuss how they would apply each DMAIC phase
to this case.

2. Discussion Points:
   ○ What would they define as the problem?
   ○ What metrics would they measure to understand
   current performance?
   ○ What might be some possible root causes?

Define, Measure, Analyse, Improve, Control

- What changes would they try to improve the discharge time?
- How would they control the process to maintain the improvement?

Outcome: Participants should come away with a stronger understanding of how DMAIC works in a real-world setting and how each phase builds on the previous one to drive improvement.

Key Takeaways from Module 2

1. DMAIC is a structured framework for identifying problems, finding root causes, implementing solutions, and sustaining improvements.
2. Each phase has a specific purpose: Define identifies the problem, Measure collects data, Analyse finds causes, Improve implements solutions, and Control ensures lasting results.
3. DMAIC can be applied to any process: From customer service and healthcare to manufacturing and service industries, DMAIC is versatile and effective.

Define, Measure, Analyse, Improve, Control

Module 3: Key Six Sigma Concepts

---

1. Critical to Quality (CTQ)

Definition:
CTQ stands for Critical to Quality. These are the specific elements that are most important to the customer, such as speed, accuracy, or durability. CTQs help teams identify which aspects of a product or service must meet a certain standard to ensure customer satisfaction.

How to Identify CTQs:
CTQs vary depending on the type of product or service, but they are generally identified by understanding what customers expect and value. In Six Sigma, CTQs provide a way to focus improvement efforts on the factors that matter most to customers.

Examples of CTQs:

- In a Restaurant: CTQs might include food quality, quick service, and order accuracy.
- In Healthcare: CTQs could include accurate diagnosis, short wait times, and clear communication.
- In Manufacturing: CTQs might focus on product durability, defect-free production, and reliable delivery times.

Importance of CTQ:
Understanding CTQs ensures that Six Sigma projects

Define, Measure, Analyse, Improve, Control

address the customer's needs and expectations, leading to improved satisfaction and loyalty.

Activity:
Ask participants to think of their own workplace or a recent customer experience they had. What do they think would be considered "critical to quality" for that product or service?

---

2. Defects and Variation

Definition of Defects:
A defect is any instance where a product or service doesn't meet the required standards or expectations set by the customer. For instance, in a call centre, a defect might be a missed call, while in a bakery, a defect could be a burnt loaf of bread.

Definition of Variation:
Variation refers to the differences or inconsistencies in a process. Variation can lead to unpredictable results, which are not ideal in any business environment. For example, if a car manufacturer's paint process varies too much, some cars might have an uneven coat, leading to defects.

Types of Variation:

- Common Cause Variation: This is natural variation that occurs regularly within a process. It's often minor and doesn't greatly affect the process.

Define, Measure, Analyse, Improve, Control

- Special Cause Variation: This is unexpected variation caused by specific issues, such as equipment failure or human error. Special cause variation often signals a problem that needs fixing.

Importance of Reducing Variation:
Reducing variation is crucial because it leads to consistency, which is a cornerstone of quality. Inconsistent processes lead to defects and unhappy customers.

Example:
Imagine a bank aiming for a standard customer service response time of under 5 minutes. If some customers wait only 3 minutes while others wait 10 minutes, this variation impacts customer satisfaction. By reducing variation and keeping wait times consistent, the bank can improve customer experience.

Activity:
Ask participants to think of a process they use regularly and to list potential sources of variation. Discuss how reducing this variation could lead to more predictable results.

---

3. Process Mapping

Definition:
Process mapping is a visual representation of the steps involved in a process, showing each stage from start to finish. It helps teams understand the flow of a process,

Define, Measure, Analyse, Improve, Control

identify bottlenecks, and spot areas where improvements can be made.

Purpose of Process Mapping:

- Understand the Current Process: Helps identify each step, task, or decision point in a process.
- Identify Waste or Delays: Reveals unnecessary steps, redundancies, or delays that slow down the process.
- Set the Stage for Improvement: Provides a clear picture of where changes can be implemented to improve efficiency and quality.

How to Create a Process Map:

1. List Each Step: Identify every step involved in the process. For example, in processing an order, the steps could include receiving the order, confirming stock, packing, and shipping.
2. Use Visual Symbols: Common symbols include ovals for start/end points, rectangles for tasks, and diamonds for decisions.
3. Connect the Steps: Draw arrows to show the sequence and flow from one step to the next.

Example:
In a hospital, a process map for patient intake might start with "Check-In" and go through steps like "Assign Room," "Initial Assessment," and "Doctor Consultation." By mapping this process, the hospital can spot delays (such as bottlenecks in assigning rooms) and look for ways to reduce patient wait times.

Define, Measure, Analyse, Improve, Control

Activity:
Have participants create a simple process map for an everyday activity, like preparing for a meeting or making coffee. This will give them hands-on practice in understanding and identifying steps in a process.

---

4. The 5 Whys – Root Cause Analysis Tool

Definition:
The 5 Whys is a simple tool that helps identify the root cause of a problem by asking "Why?" multiple times. By going deeper with each "Why," teams can uncover the underlying issues, rather than just treating symptoms.

How to Use the 5 Whys:

1. Identify the Problem: Start with a clear statement of the problem.
2. Ask "Why?": Ask why the problem is happening.
3. Continue Asking "Why?": Each answer leads to the next question, moving closer to the root cause.
4. Stop When the Root Cause is Found: Usually, after five questions, the underlying cause becomes clear.

Example:
Imagine a factory where machines frequently break down:

1. Why are the machines breaking down? – Because they aren't maintained regularly.
2. Why aren't they maintained? – Because there is no maintenance schedule.

Define, Measure, Analyse, Improve, Control

3. Why is there no schedule? – Because the company doesn't have a maintenance policy.
4. Why is there no policy? – Because there's no designated role for equipment maintenance.
5. Why is there no designated role? – Because maintenance was previously done only when a breakdown occurred.

Root Cause: No proactive maintenance policy or role, leading to frequent breakdowns. This root cause can now be addressed by creating a maintenance schedule and assigning responsibility.

Activity:
Have participants practice the 5 Whys with a common problem, such as "My workspace is often cluttered." Encourage them to uncover underlying issues and brainstorm potential solutions.

---

5. Pareto Principle (80/20 Rule)

Definition:
The Pareto Principle, often called the 80/20 rule, states that in many cases, roughly 80% of problems come from 20% of causes. By identifying and focusing on those top causes, Six Sigma teams can make a big impact with targeted improvements.

How to Use the Pareto Principle in Six Sigma:

• Identify the Most Frequent Issues: List all possible causes of a problem, and record how often each occurs.

Define, Measure, Analyse, Improve, Control

- Prioritise Efforts: Focus on the small number of causes that are responsible for the majority of issues.
- Use Pareto Charts: A Pareto chart visually displays causes in descending order of frequency, making it easy to see where to focus efforts.

Example:
A customer service team notices that most complaints are due to a few recurring issues: long wait times, unhelpful responses, and call dropouts. By focusing on just these top issues, they can solve the bulk of the problems and significantly improve customer satisfaction.

Activity:
Ask participants to think of a recurring issue in their own area (e.g., delays, errors). List possible causes and discuss which causes seem to account for most of the problem. This will help them understand the Pareto Principle and how focusing on key causes can lead to big improvements.

Summary of Key Concepts in Module 3

1. Critical to Quality (CTQ): These are the elements that are essential to meeting customer expectations. CTQs help teams focus on what matters most to the customer.
2. Defects and Variation: Defects occur when a product or service doesn't meet standards, and variation is the inconsistency that leads to defects. Reducing variation creates consistent, high-quality results.

Define, Measure, Analyse, Improve, Control

3. Process Mapping: A tool for visualising and understanding every step in a process, allowing teams to spot areas for improvement.
4. The 5 Whys: A root cause analysis tool that helps teams drill down to the underlying cause of a problem by asking "Why?" multiple times.
5. Pareto Principle (80/20 Rule): A principle stating that 80% of problems come from 20% of causes, helping teams focus on the top issues to maximise improvement impact.

Activity for Module 3: Applying Key Concepts to Everyday Scenarios

Objective: Have participants apply these key concepts to familiar situations, helping them see how Six Sigma tools can be used in daily work.

Instructions:

1. Divide participants into small groups.
2. Give each group a scenario (e.g., improving the speed of responding to emails, reducing errors in order taking).
3. Ask each group to identify CTQs, potential sources of variation, and use the 5 Whys or Pareto Principle to understand the issue.

Example Scenario: A team in a retail store notices that many products are frequently out of stock. The group could:

- Identify CTQs (e.g., product availability).

Define, Measure, Analyse, Improve, Control

- List possible causes of stockouts (e.g., delays in ordering, inaccurate forecasts).
- Use the 5 Whys to find the root cause.
- Apply the Pareto Principle to focus on the most frequent causes of stockouts.

Define, Measure, Analyse, Improve, Control

Module 4: Basic Six Sigma Tools

---

1. Check Sheets

Definition:
A Check Sheet is a simple data collection tool used to record the frequency of specific events, defects, or issues as they occur. It's often structured as a table where you can tick boxes or mark occurrences to keep track of information in real time.

Purpose of Check Sheets:

- Collect and organise data in a structured way.
- Identify patterns or trends over time.
- Provide an easy, quick way to collect data for analysis.

Example:
Imagine a hospital wants to track reasons for patient complaints. They could use a Check Sheet to list possible reasons (e.g., wait time, cleanliness, noise) and tick a box each time a specific complaint is recorded. Over time, the hospital can see which issues are the most common.

Activity:
Ask participants to think of a task in their own work where they could use a Check Sheet. Have them list common issues or steps in the task, then create a basic Check Sheet they could use to monitor those issues.

Define, Measure, Analyse, Improve, Control

2. Histograms

Definition:
A Histogram is a type of bar graph that displays the frequency distribution of data. It shows how often data points fall within a certain range, making it easy to visualise the spread or distribution of data.

Purpose of Histograms:

- Show how data is distributed (e.g., does most data cluster around a specific value, or is it spread out?).
- Identify patterns, such as whether a process tends to produce certain outcomes more frequently than others.
- Reveal variation in a process, showing if data is skewed or if it falls within an acceptable range.

Example:
A restaurant tracks how long customers wait for their orders. Using a Histogram, they find that most customers wait between 5–10 minutes, but some wait up to 20 minutes. The restaurant can then focus on reducing these longer wait times.

Activity:
Provide a sample data set, such as customer wait times at a café, and ask participants to create a simple Histogram. This will help them see how data can reveal patterns that might not be obvious from raw numbers.

3. Control Charts

Definition:
A Control Chart is a graph used to monitor the stability of a process over time. It shows data points in time order and includes a central line (average), as well as upper and lower control limits to highlight when the process may be going out of control.

Purpose of Control Charts:

- Track how a process performs over time to identify trends or shifts.
- Detect unusual patterns, such as sudden increases or decreases, that might signal issues.
- Determine if a process is consistent (in control) or if special causes are leading to variation (out of control).

Example:
In a call centre, a Control Chart might track the number of calls answered per hour. If the data points stay within the control limits, the process is stable. However, if the number drops below the lower limit, it could indicate an issue, such as not enough staff on hand.

Activity:
Provide participants with sample data, such as daily product defect counts, and ask them to plot it on a Control Chart. Discuss how they would interpret a data point that falls outside the control limits.

4. Pareto Charts

Definition:
A Pareto Chart is a bar graph that displays causes or issues in descending order of frequency, often combined with a line graph that shows cumulative percentages. It helps identify the "vital few" causes that contribute most to a problem, based on the 80/20 rule.

Purpose of Pareto Charts:

- Highlight the main contributors to a problem, allowing teams to focus on the most significant issues.
- Simplify decision-making by showing where efforts will have the most impact.
- Show the cumulative effect of each cause, revealing how addressing top causes can dramatically improve results.

Example:
A car repair shop uses a Pareto Chart to track reasons for customer complaints. They find that 80% of complaints come from just two issues: wait times and service quality. By focusing on these areas, they can make significant improvements in customer satisfaction.

Activity:
Have participants brainstorm common issues in a hypothetical scenario (e.g., reasons for missed deadlines in a project team). Ask them to rank these issues and draw a simple Pareto Chart to see which causes are most significant.

Define, Measure, Analyse, Improve, Control

5. Process Flow Diagrams

Definition:
A Process Flow Diagram (also known as a flowchart) visually maps the steps in a process, showing the sequence of tasks and decisions. Each task is represented by a shape, such as rectangles for tasks and diamonds for decisions, with arrows showing the process flow.

Purpose of Process Flow Diagrams:

- Help team members understand the sequence of steps in a process.
- Identify unnecessary steps or bottlenecks that could be eliminated to improve efficiency.
- Provide a shared visual reference that makes it easier for teams to discuss and improve a process.

How to Create a Process Flow Diagram:

1. Define the Start and End Points: What triggers the process, and where does it end?
2. List Each Step in Order: Break down the tasks in sequence.
3. Add Decision Points: Identify where decisions affect the next steps (e.g., "Is the order complete?").
4. Draw the Diagram: Use standard shapes to represent steps (rectangles) and decisions (diamonds).

Example:
A retail store uses a Process Flow Diagram to map the

steps for restocking shelves. The diagram includes steps like "Check Inventory," "Place Order," and "Stock Shelves." By visualising this process, the team can identify areas to reduce time and improve restocking speed.

Activity:
Ask participants to create a simple Process Flow Diagram for an everyday task, such as responding to a customer email or ordering office supplies. This will help them practice visualising processes and identifying possible improvements.

Key Takeaways from Module 4

1. Check Sheets: These allow for simple, structured data collection and help identify patterns in real time.
2. Histograms: A useful tool for visualising data distribution, revealing variation in a process.
3. Control Charts: Help monitor a process over time, showing when it's stable or if something is causing variation.
4. Pareto Charts: Based on the 80/20 rule, Pareto Charts help teams focus on the most significant causes of a problem.
5. Process Flow Diagrams: Provide a visual map of a process, helping teams understand the sequence of steps and identify areas for improvement.

Activity for Module 4: Tool Application Scenario

Define, Measure, Analyse, Improve, Control

Objective: Have participants apply these tools to a real-world scenario, understanding when and how each tool would be most useful.

Scenario:

- A small business wants to reduce the number of complaints it receives about delayed deliveries.

Instructions:

1. Divide participants into small groups and ask them to think about which tools they might use in this scenario.
2. Discuss Tool Application:
   o Check Sheet: Could be used to track the frequency of different delay reasons.
   o Histogram: Could display delivery times to see if there's a wide variation.
   o Control Chart: Could track delivery times over time to see if delays are consistent or random.
   o Pareto Chart: Could highlight the top reasons for delays (e.g., traffic, packaging errors).
   o Process Flow Diagram: Could map the delivery process to identify bottlenecks or unnecessary steps.

Outcome: Participants should come away with a clearer understanding of each tool's purpose and how to choose the appropriate tool based on the type of data they need to collect or analyse.

Define, Measure, Analyse, Improve, Control

Module 5: The Role of White Belts in Six Sigma

1. Understanding the White Belt Role in Six Sigma Projects

Overview of White Belt Responsibilities:
White Belts play an essential supportive role in Six Sigma projects. They are often the "eyes and ears" on the ground, gathering information, assisting with basic data collection, and providing valuable insights about day-to-day processes. Although White Belts are not project leaders, their contributions help identify improvement opportunities and support project implementation.

Key Responsibilities of White Belts:

- Collecting Data: Gathering information on specific metrics that relate to the project. This may include tracking time, frequency, or errors in a process.
- Observing and Reporting: White Belts observe daily operations and report any issues, variations, or improvement ideas to higher-level belts, such as Yellow or Green Belts.
- Supporting Change Implementation: Assisting in the implementation of changes or improvements within their work area.
- Promoting Six Sigma Culture: White Belts help foster a culture of continuous improvement by identifying small improvements in their tasks.

Define, Measure, Analyse, Improve, Control

Real-World Example: In a retail store, White Belts might help collect data on customer wait times at the checkout line. They could also note common customer issues, such as a recurring question or complaint, and report these findings to a Six Sigma project team looking to improve customer service.

---

2. Supporting Higher-Level Belts

Overview of Yellow, Green, Black, and Master Black Belts:
Understanding the role of higher-level belts helps White Belts see where they fit into the Six Sigma hierarchy.

- Yellow Belts assist with projects and may lead smaller initiatives.
- Green Belts lead projects within their functional areas, focusing on data analysis and improvement implementation.
- Black Belts manage cross-functional projects, providing advanced problem-solving expertise.
- Master Black Belts oversee Six Sigma deployment at an organisational level, providing mentorship and strategic alignment.

How White Belts Support Higher-Level Belts:

- Providing Data: White Belts gather and record data that Yellow and Green Belts need for project analysis.
- Offering Frontline Insights: As the ones closest to the process, White Belts can provide valuable information

Define, Measure, Analyse, Improve, Control

about day-to-day operations, issues, and customer feedback.

- Assisting in Communication: White Belts help communicate Six Sigma changes or updates to their team members, supporting smooth implementation.

Example of Support:
A White Belt in a call centre might track call volume and response times. This data allows a Green Belt leading a project to improve response times to analyse trends and develop solutions.

---

3. Collecting and Organising Data

Why Data Collection Matters:
Data is the foundation of Six Sigma projects, helping to define, measure, and improve processes. White Belts play a crucial role in collecting accurate data, which informs decisions made by higher-level belts.

Types of Data White Belts May Collect:

- Process Timing: Measuring how long specific tasks take to identify delays or inefficiencies.
- Error Tracking: Recording defects, errors, or issues that occur in a process.
- Customer Feedback: Documenting customer comments or complaints to understand their concerns.

Example of Data Collection:
In a manufacturing environment, White Belts might record how often defects occur on a production line,

Define, Measure, Analyse, Improve, Control

noting the time, place, and type of defect. This data can then be analysed by higher-level belts to identify root causes.

Best Practices for Data Collection:

1. Be Consistent: Record data consistently using the same methods, units, and intervals.
2. Stay Objective: Avoid making assumptions or altering data. Record facts as they are.
3. Use Check Sheets: Check Sheets provide a simple way to track data, making it easy to organise and analyse later.

Activity:
Ask participants to create a simple Check Sheet to track a common issue in their work area. This exercise will give them hands-on experience in collecting structured data.

4. Observing Processes and Identifying Improvement Opportunities

Importance of Observation:
As frontline employees, White Belts are often closest to the processes that need improvement. By observing processes and workflows, they can identify inefficiencies, bottlenecks, or recurring issues.

How to Identify Improvement Opportunities:

1. Look for Delays: Are there steps in the process where people or tasks are frequently waiting?

Define, Measure, Analyse, Improve, Control

2. Identify Common Errors: Are there certain errors or defects that happen frequently?
3. Consider Customer Feedback: What are common complaints or suggestions from customers?
4. Note Redundant Steps: Are there tasks that seem repetitive or unnecessary?

Example of Observation:
In a restaurant, a White Belt might notice that orders take longer when certain items are ordered, leading to longer wait times for customers. They could report this observation to a Six Sigma team for further investigation.

Activity:
Ask participants to observe a simple process in their work area (e.g., a routine task) and list any inefficiencies they notice. Encourage them to think about small changes that could make the process smoother.

5. Supporting Implementation of Improvements

Role of White Belts in Implementation:
White Belts often assist with implementing changes within their work area. This may include adopting new procedures, helping train colleagues on improvements, and ensuring that changes are followed.

Ways White Belts Support Implementation:

- Participating in Pilots: White Belts may be involved in pilot programs that test new procedures or tools before they're implemented widely.
- Adapting to New Procedures: They play a key role in adopting and normalising changes, setting an example for their team.
- Providing Feedback: White Belts can report on how changes impact day-to-day operations, noting any issues or adjustments needed.

Example:
If a Six Sigma project introduces a new tool for tracking inventory, White Belts might help test the tool, provide feedback on its usability, and support their teammates in learning how to use it.

Activity:
Have participants discuss a recent change in their workplace. How could White Belts support such a change? This activity helps them understand the value of their role in making improvements stick.

6. Promoting a Culture of Continuous Improvement

Continuous Improvement Mindset:
A continuous improvement mindset means always looking for small, meaningful changes that can improve quality, reduce errors, or increase efficiency. White Belts help create a culture of continuous improvement by

Define, Measure, Analyse, Improve, Control

noticing issues and suggesting ways to make their tasks easier or better.

How White Belts Contribute to Continuous Improvement:

- Adopting Small Changes: White Belts don't need to lead large projects to make a difference. They can implement small changes within their work area that improve daily tasks.
- Encouraging Team Involvement: By embracing Six Sigma principles, White Belts can inspire their peers to get involved and suggest improvements.
- Reporting Issues Promptly: White Belts should feel empowered to report issues and suggest solutions, which helps identify problems early on.

Example of Continuous Improvement:
In an office setting, a White Belt might notice that their team spends too much time searching for files. By suggesting a new file-naming convention or storage system, they help the team save time, which contributes to a more efficient process.

Activity:
Ask participants to think of one small improvement they could make in their work area. Have them share their ideas, fostering a mindset of continuous improvement.

---

7. Communication and Collaboration

Importance of Communication in Six Sigma:
Good communication is essential for successful Six Sigma projects. White Belts play a key role in relaying information between frontline staff and Six Sigma project teams.

How White Belts Communicate Effectively:

- Provide Clear Observations: When reporting an issue, be specific about what happened, when, and where.
- Be Open to Feedback: White Belts may receive feedback or suggestions from higher-level belts, so it's important to stay open to learning.
- Ask Questions: White Belts should feel comfortable asking questions about changes, project goals, or their own role.

Example of Effective Communication:
A White Belt in a call centre might report to their supervisor that calls are frequently dropped during a specific time of day. By clearly communicating this issue, they help the team investigate the cause and potentially prevent future dropped calls.

Activity:
Have participants practice explaining an issue or observation in a clear, specific way. This reinforces the importance of effective communication within Six Sigma.

Key Takeaways from Module 5

Define, Measure, Analyse, Improve, Control

1. White Belts support Six Sigma projects by collecting data, observing processes, and providing valuable frontline insights.
2. They assist higher-level belts by gathering data, suggesting improvements, and supporting implementation efforts.
3. White Belts contribute to a culture of continuous improvement by embracing small changes and encouraging team involvement.
4. Good communication is essential, helping ensure that issues are reported, improvements are understood, and feedback is provided.

Activity for Module 5: White Belt Contribution Planning

Objective: Help participants identify ways they can support Six Sigma initiatives in their own roles.

Instructions:

1. Ask participants to list one area in their work that could benefit from improvement.
2. Have them think through how they could use their White Belt knowledge to support improvement in this area, whether through data collection, observation, or suggesting a small change.

Example Responses:

- A participant in retail might say, "I could start tracking customer complaints to identify common issues and report these patterns to my supervisor."

- A participant in manufacturing could say, "I can observe how long each step takes on the production line and note any delays."

Define, Measure, Analyse, Improve, Control

Module 6: Introduction to Six Sigma Culture

---

1. Six Sigma as a Cultural Change

Definition of Six Sigma Culture:
Six Sigma culture is a way of thinking that prioritises quality, efficiency, and continuous improvement in every aspect of an organisation. It is built on the idea that processes can always be improved, and that improvements lead to better quality, lower costs, and higher customer satisfaction.

Characteristics of a Six Sigma Culture:

- Focus on Quality and Consistency: Six Sigma culture strives for high standards in every task, process, and product.
- Data-Driven Decision Making: Decisions are made based on facts and data, not assumptions.
- Commitment to Continuous Improvement: There's always room for improvement, no matter how well a process seems to work.
- Involvement of All Employees: Six Sigma encourages participation from all levels of the organisation, from frontline staff to executives.

Example:
A Six Sigma culture in a bank might mean that everyone, from tellers to managers, looks for ways to make customer interactions smoother and faster, whether by

54

Define, Measure, Analyse, Improve, Control

reducing wait times, improving the accuracy of transactions, or streamlining services.

Activity:
Ask participants to think of one area in their workplace where quality or efficiency could be improved. Discuss how a Six Sigma approach might bring positive changes to this area.

---

2. Key Principles of Six Sigma Culture

Principle 1: Customer Focus
The primary focus of Six Sigma is on delivering value to the customer. Every improvement aims to enhance the customer experience, whether that's by improving product quality, reducing wait times, or making processes more reliable.

How Customer Focus is Demonstrated:

- Understanding Customer Needs: Identifying what's critical to quality (CTQ) for the customer, such as fast service or a defect-free product.
- Measuring Customer Satisfaction: Using feedback or surveys to ensure that improvements align with customer expectations.

Example:
In a restaurant, a customer-focused Six Sigma approach might focus on reducing wait times for orders, improving food quality, or ensuring accurate orders to keep customers satisfied.

Define, Measure, Analyse, Improve, Control

Principle 2: Data-Driven Decision Making
In Six Sigma, decisions are based on data and facts, not assumptions or opinions. Data provides objective insights, allowing teams to identify root causes of problems and measure improvements.

How Data-Driven Decision Making is Demonstrated:

- Collecting Accurate Data: Using tools like check sheets or surveys to collect data on processes.
- Analysing Data: Reviewing data to find patterns or identify causes of variation in processes.
- Tracking Improvements: Using data to monitor improvements and confirm that changes are effective.

Example:
In a warehouse, data might be used to track order fulfilment times. If the data shows certain times of day with frequent delays, teams can address staffing or procedural issues to reduce delays.

Principle 3: Continuous Improvement Mindset
Continuous improvement means always looking for ways to make processes better, even after initial improvements have been made. This mindset drives ongoing progress and helps prevent stagnation.

How Continuous Improvement is Demonstrated:

Define, Measure, Analyse, Improve, Control

- Regular Reviews: Periodically reviewing processes to look for new opportunities to improve.
- Encouraging Employee Suggestions: Giving employees the freedom to suggest small changes that can improve efficiency or quality.
- Tracking Long-Term Progress: Using data to measure long-term changes and assess ongoing improvement.

Example:
In a call centre, continuous improvement might mean tracking call handling times and finding new ways to reduce them, even if the initial target has been met.

Principle 4: Collaboration and Teamwork
Six Sigma projects require collaboration across departments and roles. Everyone, from White Belts to Black Belts, plays a part in identifying and solving problems. Teamwork is crucial for achieving meaningful improvements.

How Collaboration is Demonstrated:

- Cross-Functional Teams: Team members from different departments work together on projects.
- Open Communication: Sharing information and updates regularly with all team members.
- Supporting Each Other: Everyone helps ensure changes are implemented smoothly, with everyone understanding their role in the project.

Example:
In a hospital, improving patient wait times might

involve doctors, nurses, reception staff, and even IT teams working together to streamline processes, improve communication, and reduce bottlenecks.

Activity:
Have participants discuss an improvement idea that would require collaboration across departments. Encourage them to think about who they would need to work with and what challenges might arise.

---

3. Building Confidence in Six Sigma

Helping White Belts Feel Empowered:
White Belts may feel that their role in Six Sigma is small, but their observations, data collection, and insights are critical to success. Six Sigma encourages White Belts to take an active role in identifying issues and suggesting improvements.

How White Belts Can Contribute:

- Making Small Improvements: White Belts can look for small ways to improve their own tasks, such as organising their workspace or suggesting an efficiency improvement.
- Reporting Issues: White Belts should feel empowered to report process issues they encounter or observe.
- Staying Curious: By asking questions and learning about processes, White Belts gain a better understanding of how they can make a difference.

Example of White Belt Contribution:
In a retail store, a White Belt might notice that customers frequently have questions about where to find items. They could suggest improved signage or layout changes, helping to enhance the customer experience with a small improvement.

---

4. Key Practices for Promoting Six Sigma Culture

Practice 1: Setting Personal Improvement Goals
Encourage White Belts to set small improvement goals within their own work area. Even minor changes, like reorganising a workspace or reducing time spent on repetitive tasks, contribute to a culture of continuous improvement.

Practice 2: Documenting Observations
White Belts should be encouraged to keep a record of any issues, errors, or improvement ideas they come across. This documentation can be useful when it's time to analyse processes or report to higher-level belts.

Practice 3: Participating in Team Meetings
White Belts can play an active role in team meetings by sharing observations and ideas for improvement. They can help make meetings more productive by providing insights into the daily operations that higher-level belts may not see firsthand.

Practice 4: Providing Feedback
Encouraging open communication allows White Belts to

Define, Measure, Analyse, Improve, Control

share feedback on new changes or procedures. This feedback is crucial to ensuring that implemented changes work well in practice.

Example:
In a shipping department, a White Belt might observe that packing materials are stored too far from the packing station, causing delays. They could suggest moving materials closer to save time. Their feedback can prompt improvements that make the process more efficient.

5. Reinforcing a Positive, Improvement-Focused Culture

How White Belts Can Reinforce Six Sigma Culture:

- Adopting a Problem-Solving Attitude: Rather than seeing issues as setbacks, White Belts can look at problems as opportunities to improve.
- Encouraging Colleagues: White Belts can promote Six Sigma by sharing what they've learnt and encouraging their teammates to adopt an improvement-focused mindset.
- Celebrating Small Wins: Recognising and celebrating small improvements, even incremental ones, reinforces a positive attitude toward change and improvement.

Example of Culture-Building:
In an office, a White Belt might suggest that the team track and celebrate each time a new efficiency improvement is implemented, such as saving time on

Define, Measure, Analyse, Improve, Control

filing or responding to customer inquiries. This kind of recognition can make everyone more enthusiastic about contributing to Six Sigma initiatives.

Activity:
Ask participants to list two or three ways they could personally support a Six Sigma culture in their workplace, even if their role in a project is small. Discuss how these small contributions can make a difference in fostering an improvement-oriented environment.

Key Takeaways from Module 6

1. Six Sigma culture is focused on quality, customer satisfaction, and continuous improvement.
2. Key principles of Six Sigma culture include customer focus, data-driven decisions, continuous improvement, and teamwork.
3. White Belts play a valuable role in promoting Six Sigma culture by setting personal improvement goals, reporting issues, and sharing observations.
4. Creating a Six Sigma culture requires the involvement and support of all employees, and White Belts contribute by supporting and sustaining positive change in their work areas.

Activity for Module 6: Creating a Six Sigma Culture Plan

Define, Measure, Analyse, Improve, Control

Objective: Help participants plan ways to support Six Sigma culture in their own work.

Instructions:

1. Ask participants to create a brief plan detailing specific actions they can take to promote Six Sigma culture in their area. This might include setting an improvement goal, discussing Six Sigma with team members, or sharing ideas in team meetings.
2. Have participants share their plans with the group, reinforcing the idea that everyone plays a role in building a Six Sigma culture.

Example Plans:

- A participant might decide to track customer complaints and report trends to their manager.
- Another might set a goal to find one way each week to make their tasks more efficient, such as reducing email response times or organising their workspace.

Define, Measure, Analyse, Improve, Control

Module 7: Summary and Next Steps

1. Review of Key Six Sigma Concepts

Objective: Reinforce the foundational principles and tools covered in previous modules, ensuring participants feel confident in their understanding and application of Six Sigma at the White Belt level.

Key Concepts Recap:

1. What is Six Sigma?

- Six Sigma is a data-driven methodology that aims to improve quality and efficiency by reducing defects and variation in processes.
- The primary goal is to meet customer expectations consistently, using a structured approach to problem-solving.

2. DMAIC Process

- Define: Identifying the problem, setting goals, and understanding customer requirements.
- Measure: Collecting data to understand the current state of the process.
- Analyse: Identifying the root causes of the problem.
- Improve: Implementing solutions to address root causes.
- Control: Ensuring improvements are maintained over time.

3. Key Six Sigma Tools

- Check Sheets for data collection.
- Histograms to visualise data distribution.

Define, Measure, Analyse, Improve, Control

- Control Charts for tracking process stability over time.
- Pareto Charts to focus on the most significant causes of issues.
- Process Flow Diagrams to map out and understand process steps.

4. Six Sigma Culture

- Six Sigma culture is focused on quality, continuous improvement, teamwork, and data-driven decisions.
- White Belts play a vital role by collecting data, observing processes, and supporting improvements.

Activity:
Have participants complete a brief quiz or reflection exercise where they summarise each concept in their own words, helping to reinforce what they've learnt.

---

2. Applying Six Sigma in Daily Work

Objective: Help participants see how they can use their White Belt knowledge to improve processes and support Six Sigma projects within their own work areas.

Applying Key Concepts:

1. Identifying Improvement Opportunities
White Belts should start by observing their daily tasks and identifying areas that could be improved. For example, if they notice frequent delays or repetitive tasks, they might suggest solutions to streamline those processes.

2. Data Collection and Observation
White Belts can apply their knowledge of data collection by using Check Sheets to record occurrences of specific issues, timing certain tasks, or tracking common problems. This data can then be shared with their team to provide insights and guide improvements.

3. Using Six Sigma Tools

- Check Sheets for tracking issues or delays.
- Histograms for displaying data and identifying patterns.
- Pareto Charts for prioritising the most frequent issues.
- 5 Whys to identify root causes of recurring problems.

Example:
In an office setting, a White Belt could use a Check Sheet to track how many times a printer error occurs each week. This data could help the team understand the frequency of the problem and identify if a maintenance check or a replacement is needed.

Activity:
Ask participants to write down one task in their role where they could apply a Six Sigma tool to improve efficiency or quality. Encourage them to think about data they could collect or process steps they could simplify.

3. Setting Personal Improvement Goals

Define, Measure, Analyse, Improve, Control

Objective: Empower participants to take small, meaningful steps toward improvement in their own roles, reinforcing a Six Sigma mindset.

Goal-Setting Process:

1. Identify an Area for Improvement: Choose a task or process they are involved in regularly.
2. Set a Measurable Goal: Create a simple, achievable goal that can be measured, such as reducing time spent on a task by 10%.
3. Apply Six Sigma Tools: Decide which Six Sigma tools (like a Check Sheet or Process Flow Diagram) can help achieve this goal.
4. Monitor Progress: Track improvements over time, adjusting as needed to achieve the desired outcome.

Example of a Personal Improvement Goal:
A White Belt working in customer service might set a goal to reduce call resolution time by 5%. They could use a Check Sheet to track call times and then look for patterns or causes of longer calls, identifying ways to handle common issues more efficiently.

Activity:
Have participants write down one specific improvement goal they would like to achieve in their role over the next month. They should include how they'll measure success and which tools they might use.

---

4. Advancing to Yellow Belt

Objective: Provide an overview of the Yellow Belt level in Six Sigma and encourage participants to consider advancing their skills.

Overview of Yellow Belt Responsibilities:

- Leading Small-Scale Projects: Yellow Belts can take on small projects within their work area, using DMAIC to drive improvements.
- Supporting Green and Black Belts: Yellow Belts provide data, insights, and assistance in larger projects led by higher-level belts.
- Gaining a Deeper Understanding of Six Sigma Tools: Yellow Belts learn more advanced tools for data analysis and process improvement.

Benefits of Advancing to Yellow Belt:

- Increased Responsibility: Yellow Belts have more involvement in Six Sigma projects, often taking on a leadership role within their department.
- Improved Problem-Solving Skills: Gaining deeper knowledge of Six Sigma tools helps Yellow Belts solve more complex issues.
- Career Advancement: Six Sigma certification is valuable in many industries, helping employees advance their careers.

Activity:
Have participants discuss or reflect on whether they'd like to pursue a Yellow Belt, and ask them to consider what additional skills or knowledge they hope to gain. This can help them plan their professional development path.

Define, Measure, Analyse, Improve, Control

5. Creating a Personal Action Plan

Objective: Help participants create a plan for applying Six Sigma principles and achieving continuous improvement in their roles.

Steps to Creating a Personal Action Plan:

1. Identify Immediate Applications: Choose one or two ways they can apply what they've learnt right away, such as using a Check Sheet or observing processes.
2. Set Improvement Goals: Define specific, achievable goals they want to work on over the next month.
3. Monitor and Review: Decide how they'll track their progress and when they'll review the impact of these improvements.
4. Seek Feedback: Encourage participants to ask for feedback from supervisors or peers on their efforts, helping them refine their skills.

Example Action Plan: A participant working in inventory management might decide to use a Check Sheet to track stockouts and then set a goal to reduce stockouts by 20% over the next month. They'll review their progress weekly and discuss their findings with a supervisor.

Activity:
Ask participants to create a brief action plan using these steps, outlining their next steps for applying Six Sigma. This plan will help them take immediate, practical steps toward continuous improvement.

Define, Measure, Analyse, Improve, Control

6. Summary of the White Belt Journey

Recap of the White Belt Role:
White Belts provide essential support to Six Sigma teams by collecting data, observing processes, and promoting a culture of improvement. They help identify issues and implement small changes, contributing to the overall success of Six Sigma projects.

Key Takeaways:

- Six Sigma is about quality and efficiency, focused on meeting customer expectations and reducing variation.
- The DMAIC process provides a structured approach to problem-solving that White Belts can support through data collection and observation.
- Six Sigma culture encourages continuous improvement, teamwork, and data-driven decisions, all of which White Belts can promote in their daily work.

Celebrating Completion:
Congratulate participants on completing the White Belt training, highlighting the importance of their role in Six Sigma and the positive impact they can have on their teams and organisations.

7. Additional Resources for Further Learning

Define, Measure, Analyse, Improve, Control

Objective: Provide participants with resources they can use to continue learning about Six Sigma, even after the course ends.

Suggested Resources:

- Books: Recommend introductory books on Six Sigma, such as **Six Sigma for Dummies** or **The Lean Six Sigma Pocket Toolbook**.
- Online Courses: Share links to reputable online courses or certification programs, like those offered by Coursera, Udemy, or ASQ (American Society for Quality).
- Mentorship: Encourage participants to seek mentorship from a Yellow or Green Belt in their organisation if available, which can provide guidance on using Six Sigma tools effectively.

Activity:
Have participants list one or two resources they'd like to explore further, helping them create a personal development plan for building on their White Belt training.

Key Takeaways from Module 7

1. Six Sigma White Belts play a valuable role by supporting projects through data collection, observation, and promoting a culture of continuous improvement.
2. Applying Six Sigma in daily work can lead to small but meaningful improvements, contributing to quality and efficiency.

Define, Measure, Analyse, Improve, Control

3. Further learning opportunities include progressing to Yellow Belt certification or exploring additional resources to deepen Six Sigma knowledge.

Final Activity: Reflection and Sharing

Objective: Encourage participants to reflect on their learning journey and share key takeaways with the group.

Instructions:

1. Ask participants to reflect on what they found most valuable in the course and how they plan to apply it in their roles.
2. Invite participants to share their thoughts with the group, reinforcing a sense of accomplishment and readiness to support Six Sigma initiatives.

Define, Measure, Analyse, Improve, Control

6 Sigma White Belt Course Handouts

Module 1: Introduction to Six Sigma

Learning Objectives:

- Understand what Six Sigma is and why it's important for process improvement.
- Define the core concepts and terminology associated with Six Sigma.
- Familiarise with the DMAIC process.

Key Terms:

- **Six Sigma**: A data-driven methodology aimed at improving process quality by reducing defects to a level of 3.4 defects per million opportunities.
- **Defect**: A failure to meet customer requirements.
- **Variation**: Differences in process performance that lead to defects or inefficiencies.
- **Process Improvement**: Activities aimed at making a process more efficient and consistent.

Key Concepts:

1. **DMAIC Process**: The core of Six Sigma methodology, which stands for **Define, Measure, Analyse, Improve, and Control**.

Define, Measure, Analyse, Improve, Control

2. **Voice of the Customer (VoC)**: A method for collecting customer needs and ensuring that process improvements align with those needs.
3. **Critical to Quality (CTQ)**: Key characteristics or factors that are essential to meeting customer expectations.

Diagram: DMAIC Process
Here's a flowchart to visualise the DMAIC cycle.

```
In plaintext

[Define] → [Measure] → [Analyse] → [Improve] →
[Control]
```

Example: In a factory, if defects in a product (e.g., broken bottles) are detected, the Six Sigma process will be used to reduce the defect rate, identifying the causes, and making necessary improvements.

Activity:
True or False

- Six Sigma is only used in manufacturing industries. **(False)**
- The goal of Six Sigma is to reduce defects to 3.4 per million opportunities. **(True)**

Module 2: Define Phase - Understanding the Problem

Define, Measure, Analyse, Improve, Control

Learning Objectives:

- Learn how to clearly define the problem you are trying to solve in the Define phase of DMAIC.
- Understand the tools and methods used in this phase.

Key Terms:

- **Problem Statement**: A concise description of the issue to be solved.
- **Project Charter**: A document that outlines the project's objectives, scope, and team members.

Define Tools:

- **SIPOC Diagram**: A high-level map that describes the **Suppliers**, **Inputs**, **Process**, **Outputs**, and **Customers** involved in the process.

SIPOC Diagram:

```
In plaintext

Suppliers → Inputs → Process → Outputs → Customers
```

Key Concepts:

1. **Defining the Problem**: Clear understanding of the problem and its impact.

Define, Measure, Analyse, Improve, Control

2. **Goal Setting**: Define measurable goals for the project.
3. **Stakeholder Identification**: Identify all stakeholders involved, such as suppliers, employees, and customers.

Example: In a hospital, the problem statement could be: "Patients are experiencing long wait times in the emergency room." The goal is to reduce wait times by 20% in the next three months.

Activity:
Create a SIPOC Diagram for a process you're familiar with (e.g., ordering food at a restaurant). List the suppliers, inputs, process steps, outputs, and customers.

Module 3: Measure Phase - Collecting Data

Learning Objectives:

- Understand how to collect data to measure the performance of the current process.
- Learn how to define metrics and establish a baseline.

Key Terms:

- **Key Performance Indicators (KPIs)**: Metrics used to assess the effectiveness of a process.

Define, Measure, Analyse, Improve, Control

- **Baseline Data**: Initial data collected to understand the current performance of the process.

Measure Tools:

- **Data Collection Plan**: A document outlining what data is needed, how it will be collected, and how frequently.
- **Pareto Chart**: A bar chart that helps prioritise issues by showing the most frequent or impactful causes.

Pareto Chart Example:

```
In plaintext

|--------------------------------------------|
|                Top Issues for Process      |
|--------------------------------------------|
| Issue 1  | |█████████████████████████      |
| Issue 2  | |█████████████████              |
| Issue 3  | |██████████                      |
|--------------------------------------------|
```

Key Concepts:

1. **Data Collection**: Collect data that accurately reflects process performance.
2. **Defining Metrics**: Select metrics that will give insight into process efficiency and effectiveness.
3. **Measuring Performance**: Use control charts and histograms to track variations in the process.

Example: A call centre may track the number of calls answered per hour, customer satisfaction scores, and the average time spent on each call as key metrics to measure performance.

Activity:
Create a Data Collection Plan for a process you work with (e.g., customer service response times). What data would you collect, and how would you gather it?

Module 4: Analyse Phase - Identifying Root Causes

Learning Objectives:

- Learn how to use data analysis to identify the root causes of process problems.
- Apply tools like Fishbone Diagrams and the 5 Whys technique to determine root causes.

Key Terms:

- **Root Cause**: The underlying cause of a problem that, if addressed, would eliminate the issue permanently.
- **Fishbone Diagram**: A tool used to visually identify potential causes of a problem.

Fishbone Diagram:

```
In plaintext

[Problem] -->
        [People] --> [Training Issues]
        [Methods] --> [Process Variability]
        [Machines] --> [Outdated Equipment]
        [Materials] --> [Poor Quality Raw Materials]
```

Key Concepts:

1. **Root Cause Analysis**: Identify not just the symptoms but the underlying causes of problems.
2. **Data Analysis**: Use statistical methods and charts to uncover the root causes.
3. **The 5 Whys**: Ask "Why?" five times to drill down into the root cause of a problem.

Example: If a factory has defects in its products, the Fishbone Diagram might show that defective products are due to poorly trained employees, outdated equipment, or substandard materials.

Activity:
Use the 5 Whys Technique: Think of a problem at work (e.g., delays in deliveries), and ask "Why?" five times to uncover the root cause.

Module 5: Improve Phase - Implementing Solutions

Define, Measure, Analyse, Improve, Control

Learning Objectives:

- Understand how to design and implement solutions to address root causes identified in the Analyze phase.
- Learn how to pilot and test improvements before full-scale implementation.

Key Terms:

- **Solution Implementation**: Applying changes to improve the process.
- **Pilot Testing**: Running a small-scale test to validate the effectiveness of the solution.

Key Concepts:

1. **Solution Design**: Create solutions that directly address the root causes.
2. **Pilot Testing**: Test solutions on a small scale to verify their effectiveness before full implementation.
3. **Risk Management**: Anticipate and mitigate potential risks related to the solution.

Example: A call centre may implement a new call routing system to reduce wait times. A pilot test can be conducted on one team to ensure it works before rolling it out organisation-wide.

Define, Measure, Analyse, Improve, Control

Activity:
Design an Improvement Plan for a process you're familiar with. What changes would you make, and how would you test them?

Define, Measure, Analyse, Improve, Control

6 Sigma White Belt Answer Sheet

Section 1: True/False Questions

1. Six Sigma is a methodology designed to eliminate defects and improve process efficiency.

2. The DMAIC methodology is specific to the manufacturing industry only.

3. A SIPOC diagram is a tool used to map out a process and its key components.

4. In Six Sigma, "Critical to Quality" (CTQ) elements represent attributes important to the customer.

5. White Belts play a supportive role in Six Sigma projects by gathering data and assisting higher-level belts.

Section 2: Multiple Choice Questions

6. Which of the following is the primary focus of Six Sigma?

    o A) Increasing profit by any means
    o B) Reducing variation and eliminating defects
    o C) Improving employee satisfaction
    o D) Reducing time spent on projects

7. The DMAIC phases stand for:

Define, Measure, Analyse, Improve, Control

- A) Define, Measure, Adjust, Implement, Control
- B) Define, Measure, Analyse, Improve, Control
- C) Define, Map, Analyse, Integrate, Change
- D) Discover, Measure, Assess, Implement, Correct

8. A Fishbone Diagram is commonly used to:

- A) Track data over time
- B) Identify potential causes of a problem
- C) Display frequency distribution
- D) Show the sequence of steps in a process

9. In Six Sigma, the purpose of a Check Sheet is to:

- A) Track and collect data in a structured way
- B) Visualise data distribution
- C) Analyse root causes of problems
- D) Outline the steps in the DMAIC process

10. Which of the following is a responsibility of a Six Sigma White Belt?

- A) Leading large-scale Six Sigma projects
- B) Providing data and insights to higher-level belts
- C) Conducting complex statistical analysis
- D) Developing a Six Sigma project charter

Section 3: Short Answer Questions

11. Describe the main purpose of the Define phase in the DMAIC methodology.

12. Explain what "Critical to Quality" (CTQ) means in Six Sigma.

13. What is the purpose of using a Process Flow Diagram?

14. Define the role of a White Belt in supporting Six Sigma projects.

15. Why is data-driven decision-making important in Six Sigma?

Section 4: Scenario-Based Questions

16. Scenario: A White Belt is assigned to help reduce customer wait times at a retail store. What steps would they take in the Define phase to begin addressing this issue?

17. Scenario: During a Six Sigma project, a White Belt observes that most product defects occur during the packaging stage. How might they assist in identifying potential root causes of this issue?

18. Scenario: In the Measure phase of a project, a White Belt is asked to collect data on delivery times for a logistics company. Which Six Sigma tool would be useful, and how would they apply it?

19. Scenario: A White Belt is involved in a project to improve accuracy in data entry. What is one improvement approach they might suggest in the Improve phase?

Define, Measure, Analyse, Improve, Control

20. Scenario: After helping to implement a new process in the Control phase, a White Belt notices that deviations are starting to occur. How could they help ensure the process remains consistent?

Define, Measure, Analyse, Improve, Control

6 Sigma White Belt Answer Sheet

Section 1: True/False Answers

1. True – Six Sigma is a methodology that focuses on defect reduction and process improvement.

2. False – DMAIC can be applied across various industries, not just manufacturing.

3. True – A SIPOC diagram is used to map a process's Suppliers, Inputs, Process, Outputs, and Customers.

4. True – CTQ elements are attributes that matter most to the customer and are critical to quality.

5. True – White Belts support Six Sigma projects by gathering data, assisting higher-level belts, and making small improvements in their work areas.

Section 2: Multiple Choice Answers

6. B) Reducing variation and eliminating defects – The main focus of Six Sigma is to improve process quality by reducing defects and variation.

7. B) Define, Measure, Analyses, Improve, Control – DMAIC stands for Define, Measure, Analyses, Improve, and Control.

8. B) Identify potential causes of a problem – A Fishbone Diagram, also called an Ishikawa diagram, is used to brainstorm and categorise causes of a problem.

Define, Measure, Analyse, Improve, Control

9. A) Track and collect data in a structured way – Check Sheets are used to gather and organise data in a structured format for analysis.

10. B) Providing data and insights to higher-level belts – White Belts assist in data collection, reporting, and supporting the implementation of improvements.

Section 3: Short Answer Answers

11. Answer: The main purpose of the Define phase is to clearly identify the problem, set specific goals, and understand the customer's needs and project objectives.

12. Answer: CTQ, or "Critical to Quality," represents the key aspects of a product or service that are most important to the customer, ensuring that improvements focus on customer satisfaction.

13. Answer: A Process Flow Diagram visually maps the steps in a process, helping teams understand the sequence of tasks and identify potential inefficiencies or areas for improvement.

14. Answer: A White Belt supports Six Sigma projects by collecting data, observing processes, providing insights, and assisting in implementing improvements within their work area.

15. Answer: Data-driven decision-making is important because it bases improvements on actual data, ensuring solutions are targeted, measurable, and effective rather than based on assumptions.

Section 4: Scenario-Based Answers

Define, Measure, Analyse, Improve, Control

16. Answer:

- Define the problem by creating a problem statement, such as "Reduce customer wait times."
- Set measurable goals for improvement (e.g., reduce average wait time by 20%).
- Identify the stakeholders, such as store staff and customers, who are affected by the issue.

17. Answer:

- Use a Fishbone Diagram to brainstorm potential causes of defects in the packaging stage.
- Apply the 5 Whys to dig deeper into possible root causes.
- Gather data on specific types of defects to help higher-level belts analyse and address the issue.

18. Answer:

- A Check Sheet would be useful to record each delivery time and track patterns.
- The White Belt could record delivery times at different times of day or by location to identify trends in the data.

19. Answer:

- Suggest a standardised checklist or set of guidelines for data entry to reduce errors.
- Propose a training session to improve consistency in the data entry process.

20. Answer:

Define, Measure, Analyse, Improve, Control

- Use a Control Chart to monitor key metrics and detect when deviations occur.
- Regularly review the process and remind team members of the updated procedures to ensure adherence.

Define, Measure, Analyse, Improve, Control

6 sigma and 5s examples

Example 1: Boutique Hotel – Reducing Check-in Times and Organising Housekeeping Supplies

Sector: **Hospitality**

Background: A small boutique hotel faced delays in check-in times, affecting customer satisfaction. Additionally, housekeeping supplies were disorganised, leading to delays in room turnover.

Before Implementation:

- **Long Check-in Times**: Due to inefficient procedures, the check-in process took up to 15 minutes per guest.
- **Disorganised Housekeeping Supplies**: Housekeeping staff spent time searching for supplies, extending room turnover times.
- **Customer Complaints**: Guests were frustrated with the long wait to check in and with delays in room availability.

During Implementation:

- **5S Organisation of Supplies**: The hotel used 5S to organise cleaning supplies and toiletries in a central storage area. Each item was labelled, and high-use items were easily accessible.
- **Six Sigma Standardisation (DMAIC)**: The check-in process was mapped and optimised, with standardised procedures for each step, such as ID verification, payment, and key issuance.

Define, Measure, Analyse, Improve, Control

- **Employee Training**: Staff were trained in the new check-in process, and a checklist was implemented to ensure a consistent approach.

After Implementation:

- **Reduced Check-in Times**: Check-in times were reduced by 40%, leading to shorter waits for guests.
- **Improved Room Turnover**: Organised housekeeping supplies reduced room preparation time by 25%, increasing room availability.
- **Higher Customer Satisfaction**: Guests were pleased with the streamlined check-in and timely room availability, boosting the hotel's ratings.

Define, Measure, Analyse, Improve, Control

Example 2: IT Support Company – Improving Ticket Resolution and Organising Tools

Sector: IT Services

Background: An IT support company faced long resolution times for technical issues, with tools and documents disorganised across multiple locations.

Before Implementation:

- **Delayed Ticket Resolution**: Support tickets often took days to resolve due to inefficient handling.
- **Disorganised Workspaces**: Technicians had to search for tools, increasing response times.
- **Client Complaints**: Clients frequently expressed dissatisfaction with the time taken to resolve their issues.

During Implementation:

- **5S for Workspace Organisation**: Tools and documentation were organised into a centralised, labelled storage system. Technicians received designated toolkits, reducing search time.
- **DMAIC for Ticket Process Optimisation**: The team mapped the support ticket process, identifying redundant steps and streamlining troubleshooting procedures.
- **Standardised Procedures**: A standardised process for troubleshooting and documentation was introduced to ensure consistency.

After Implementation:

- **Faster Ticket Resolution**: Ticket resolution time decreased by 30%, leading to quicker support for clients.

Define, Measure, Analyse, Improve, Control

- **Organised Work Environment**: Technicians could access tools quickly, improving their efficiency.
- **Improved Client Satisfaction**: Clients experienced faster support, resulting in fewer complaints and stronger relationships with the IT firm.

Define, Measure, Analyse, Improve, Control

Example 3: Construction Company – Reducing Material Waste and Organising Job Sites

Sector: **Construction**

Background: A small construction firm encountered high material wastage and safety risks due to disorganised job sites.

Before Implementation:

- **Material Waste**: Lack of proper storage led to frequent damage and waste.
- **Safety Risks**: Tools and materials were scattered across the job site, creating safety hazards.
- **Project Delays**: Disorganisation led to delays in project timelines.

During Implementation:

- **5S Organisation of Tools and Materials**: The company designated storage areas for tools and materials, implemented colour-coded zones, and set up signs to improve organisation.
- **Six Sigma for Waste Reduction**: Using DMAIC, the company identified sources of waste, implementing a material tracking system to better forecast and control usage.
- **Safety Procedures**: Standard safety protocols were introduced, including daily clean-ups and tool inspections.

After Implementation:

- **Reduced Material Waste**: Material waste dropped by 20%, leading to cost savings.
- **Improved Safety**: The organised work environment reduced safety incidents by 30%.

Define, Measure, Analyse, Improve, Control

- **Timely Project Completion**: The reduced waste and better organisation contributed to more timely project completions.

Define, Measure, Analyse, Improve, Control

Example 4: Car Repair Shop – Streamlining Repair Process and Organising Tools

Sector: **Automotive Services**

Background: A car repair shop experienced long wait times for repairs, with disorganised tools and inventory contributing to inefficiencies.

Before Implementation:

- **Long Repair Times**: The average repair time was extended by technicians having to search for parts and tools.
- **Disorganised Workstations**: Tools were scattered, making it challenging for technicians to work efficiently.
- **Customer Dissatisfaction**: Long wait times led to low customer satisfaction.

During Implementation:

- **5S Tool Organisation**: The repair shop applied 5S to organise tools and parts based on frequency of use, with clear labelling and shadow boards.
- **Six Sigma Process Standardisation**: The repair process was mapped out, and bottlenecks were identified. Standard procedures for common repairs were implemented.
- **Employee Training**: Technicians were trained on the new setup and on following the standard repair process.

After Implementation:

- **Faster Repair Times**: Repair time reduced by 25%, allowing the shop to serve more customers daily.
- **Organised Workspace**: Technicians could quickly locate tools and parts, improving their efficiency.

Define, Measure, Analyse, Improve, Control

- **Increased Customer Satisfaction**: Faster repairs led to higher customer satisfaction and positive reviews.

Define, Measure, Analyse, Improve, Control

Example 5: App Development Start-up, Reducing Bugs and Streamlining Coding Process

Sector: Technology

Background: An app development start-up struggled with high bug rates and disorganised code repositories, leading to longer development times and project delays.

Before Implementation:

- **Frequent Bugs**: The high number of bugs required frequent debugging, delaying project completion.
- **Disorganised Repositories**: Code was not well-organised, making collaboration difficult.
- **Project Delays**: Frequent rework due to bugs pushed back release dates.

During Implementation:

- **5S for Code Organisation**: Code repositories were standardised, with a consistent file-naming system and folder structure. Version control was improved to track code changes.
- **Six Sigma for Bug Reduction**: The DMAIC process was applied to analyse and eliminate common bug sources. The team created a standard checklist for quality checks before code submission.
- **Testing and Standardisation**: Automated testing was introduced to catch bugs early in development.

After Implementation:

- **Reduced Bug Frequency**: Bug occurrence decreased by 35%, reducing time spent on debugging.

Define, Measure, Analyse, Improve, Control

- **Organised Code Repositories**: The organised code structure allowed developers to work collaboratively with fewer issues.
- **Faster Project Completion**: Improved efficiency led to quicker project completion and on-time releases.

Define, Measure, Analyse, Improve, Control

Example 6: Professional Photographer – Organising Equipment and Streamlining Editing Workflow

Sector: **Creative Services**

Background: A photographer struggled with disorganised equipment and a slow photo-editing process, which affected client delivery times.

Before Implementation:

- **Disorganised Equipment**: Cables, lenses, and memory cards were scattered, causing setup delays.
- **Slow Editing Workflow**: The lack of a structured editing process led to extended delivery times.
- **Client Dissatisfaction**: Clients often had to wait longer than expected for their photos.

During Implementation:

- **5S for Equipment Organisation**: Equipment was organised into labelled containers for easy access. Frequently used items were stored in a mobile kit for on-location shoots.
- **Six Sigma Process Standardisation**: The photographer created a standard workflow for editing, including batch processing and present application to speed up editing.
- **Backup and Version Control**: A backup system for photos was implemented, reducing the risk of lost work.

After Implementation:

- **Faster Setup and Editing**: The organised setup and structured editing process reduced turnaround time by 40%.

Define, Measure, Analyse, Improve, Control

- **Efficient Equipment Use**: Quick access to equipment enabled the photographer to work more efficiently on location.
- **Higher Client Satisfaction**: Faster delivery times improved client satisfaction and referrals.

Define, Measure, Analyse, Improve, Control

Example 7: Local Gym – Enhancing Member Experience and Equipment Maintenance

Sector: Health and Fitness

Background: A local gym faced issues with equipment availability and member complaints about disorganised spaces, impacting the user experience.

Before Implementation:

- **Unavailable Equipment**: Members often had to wait to use certain equipment during peak hours.
- **Disorganised Space**: Weights and mats were frequently left out, creating a cluttered environment.
- **Member Complaints**: Members were frustrated with the wait times and cluttered workout areas.

During Implementation:

- **5S Organisation of Equipment**: The gym designated areas for weights, mats, and machines, with signs and visual reminders. High-use equipment was placed in accessible zones.
- **Six Sigma Process Mapping**: A process was developed for cleaning, inspecting, and restocking equipment at regular intervals to ensure availability.
- **Feedback System**: A member feedback system was set up to gather insights and improve services.

After Implementation:

- **Increased Equipment Availability**: Members had quicker access to equipment, reducing wait times by 30%.
- **Organised and Clean Environment**: Clutter-free workout areas improved safety and enhanced the gym experience.

101

- **Higher Member Satisfaction**: Members appreciated the organised environment, contributing to better retention rates.

Define, Measure, Analyse, Improve, Control

Example 8: Dental Clinic – Reducing Patient Wait Times and Streamlining Equipment Usage

Sector: Healthcare

Background: A small dental clinic faced challenges with long patient wait times and inefficient equipment usage, leading to low patient satisfaction.

Before Implementation:

- **Long Wait Times**: Patients waited 20–30 minutes on average, as equipment was frequently missing or not prepped for appointments.
- **Disorganised Equipment**: Dental instruments and materials were scattered, leading to delays in preparing for each patient.
- **Patient Dissatisfaction**: Patients expressed frustration with the wait and perceived disorganisation.

During Implementation:

- **5S for Equipment Organisation**: Tools and materials were organised into standardised kits based on treatment type, and frequently used items were easily accessible.
- **DMAIC Process Standardisation**: The clinic mapped out the patient journey to identify bottlenecks and introduced standard procedures for each appointment type to reduce preparation time.

After Implementation:

- **Reduced Wait Times**: Wait times decreased by 40%, as equipment was consistently available and prepped.
- **Efficient Equipment Usage**: The organised setup improved efficiency, allowing dentists to see more patients.

Define, Measure, Analyse, Improve, Control

- **Higher Patient Satisfaction**: The clinic received positive feedback on the improved wait times and professionalism.

Example 9: Landscaping Company – Organising Equipment and Reducing Time on Job Sites

Sector: Service

Background: A small landscaping business experienced delays due to disorganised tools and equipment, affecting job completion times and client satisfaction.

Before Implementation:

- **Disorganised Tools**: Equipment was often scattered or missing from job sites, resulting in delays.
- **Extended Job Completion Times**: The lack of organisation increased time spent at each location.
- **Client Complaints**: Clients were dissatisfied with extended project durations.

During Implementation:

- **5S Organisation of Tools and Vehicles**: Trucks were organised with designated spaces for each tool, and labelled bins were used to separate equipment by job type.
- **Six Sigma for Workflow Efficiency**: A checklist was introduced for loading equipment, ensuring nothing was forgotten.

After Implementation:

- **Reduced Job Completion Times**: Job completion times decreased by 25%, enabling the team to take on more clients.
- **Improved Tool Accessibility**: Organised trucks and equipment made it easy for employees to retrieve tools, increasing productivity.

Define, Measure, Analyse, Improve, Control

- **Enhanced Client Satisfaction**: Clients were pleased with the quicker project completion and smooth workflow.

Define, Measure, Analyse, Improve, Control

Example 10: Law Office – Reducing Case Preparation Time and Improving File Organisation

Sector: Legal Services

Background: A law office struggled with long case preparation times and disorganised client files, impacting client service quality.

Before Implementation:

- **Slow Case Prep**: Case files were incomplete or disorganised, leading to long preparation times.
- **Lost Files**: Physical files were often misplaced, causing frustration and delays.
- **Client Frustration**: Clients were unhappy with the slow case progress.

During Implementation:

- **5S for Document Management**: Files were digitised and organised with consistent naming conventions, and physical files were stored alphabetically.
- **DMAIC Process for Case Preparation**: Standard procedures were developed for gathering and preparing case documents, reducing time spent searching.

After Implementation:

- **Quicker Case Prep**: Preparation times decreased by 30%, allowing attorneys to handle more cases.
- **Organised Filing System**: The digital system allowed for quicker access to documents.
- **Higher Client Satisfaction**: Improved efficiency led to fewer complaints and increased client referrals.

Define, Measure, Analyse, Improve, Control

Example 11: Spa and Wellness Centre – Improving Treatment Flow and Enhancing Inventory Management

Sector: **Health and Wellness**

Background: A small spa faced challenges with disorganised treatment rooms and inventory shortages, affecting the client experience.

Before Implementation:

- **Disorganised Supplies**: Treatment products were often misplaced, resulting in interruptions during treatments.
- **Inventory Shortages**: Essential products were frequently out of stock.
- **Client Complaints**: Clients complained about delays in treatments and product unavailability.

During Implementation:

- **5S for Supply Organisation**: Treatment rooms were standardised with labelled shelves for products, and commonly used items were placed in easy-to-reach spots.
- **Six Sigma for Inventory Management**: The spa implemented a reorder system to track stock levels, reducing shortages.

After Implementation:

- **Improved Treatment Flow**: Treatment interruptions decreased, as supplies were organised and easily accessible.
- **Reduced Shortages**: The inventory system prevented stockouts, ensuring products were always available.
- **Enhanced Client Experience**: Clients experienced uninterrupted treatments, improving overall satisfaction.

Define, Measure, Analyse, Improve, Control

Example 12: Catering Company – Streamlining Food Prep and Reducing Food Waste

Sector: **Food Services**

Background: A small catering business had issues with disorganised food prep stations and high food waste, impacting efficiency and profitability.

Before Implementation:

- **Slow Food Prep**: Disorganised workstations led to longer prep times.
- **High Food Waste**: Poor inventory control resulted in frequent spoilage and waste.
- **Customer Dissatisfaction**: Orders were sometimes delayed due to slow prep.

During Implementation:

- **5S for Kitchen Organisation**: The kitchen was reorganised with labelled areas for each food type and dedicated prep zones.
- **DMAIC for Waste Reduction**: The team analysed food usage patterns and implemented inventory checks to reduce spoilage.

After Implementation:

- **Faster Prep Times**: Food prep times decreased by 35%, enabling the team to fulfil more orders.
- **Reduced Food Waste**: Inventory control reduced spoilage, saving costs.
- **Increased Customer Satisfaction**: Orders were delivered on time, resulting in higher customer satisfaction.

Example 13: Art Studio – Organising Supplies and Improving Project Turnaround

Sector: **Creative Services**

Background: A small art studio faced challenges with disorganised supplies and slow project completion, affecting productivity and customer satisfaction.

Before Implementation:

- **Disorganised Supplies**: Art materials were scattered, making it difficult to find supplies.
- **Extended Project Times**: Disorganisation and setup delays prolonged project timelines.
- **Client Complaints**: Clients were frustrated with delays in project completion.

During Implementation:

- **5S for Supply Organisation**: Supplies were organised by type (e.g., paints, brushes) and placed in labelled drawers for easy access.
- **Standardisation of Processes (Six Sigma)**: The studio developed a standard setup procedure, reducing preparation time for each project.

After Implementation:

- **Improved Workflow**: Project setup and completion times decreased by 40%.
- **Efficient Use of Supplies**: Quick access to supplies improved productivity.
- **Higher Client Satisfaction**: Projects were completed on time, leading to positive client feedback.

Define, Measure, Analyse, Improve, Control

Example 14: Fitness Studio – Organising Equipment and Reducing Wait Times

Sector: Fitness

Background: A fitness studio faced complaints about disorganised equipment and member wait times, affecting the member experience.

Before Implementation:

- **Disorganised Equipment**: Weights and mats were scattered, causing clutter and confusion.
- **Long Wait Times**: Members often had to wait to use popular equipment.
- **Member Dissatisfaction**: Members were dissatisfied with the disorganisation and wait times.

During Implementation:

- **5S for Equipment Organisation**: Equipment was categorised and labelled with designated storage areas, making it easy for members to return items.
- **DMAIC for Equipment Usage**: Usage data was analysed to identify peak times, and equipment was repositioned for better accessibility.

After Implementation:

- **Reduced Wait Times**: Wait times decreased by 25% as members had quicker access to equipment.
- **Organised Workout Area**: The clutter-free environment improved the workout experience.
- **Higher Member Satisfaction**: Members appreciated the organised setup, resulting in positive feedback.

Define, Measure, Analyse, Improve, Control

Example 15: Florist Shop – Reducing Waste and Organising Supplies

Sector: **Retail (Floristry)**

Background: A florist shop faced high flower waste and disorganised supplies, impacting profitability and customer satisfaction.

Before Implementation:

- **High Flower Waste**: Flowers frequently wilted before use due to poor inventory management.
- **Disorganised Supplies**: Tools and materials were scattered, leading to delays.
- **Customer Complaints**: Orders were sometimes delayed due to inefficiency.

During Implementation:

- **5S for Supplies Organisation**: Supplies were organised by category, and perishable flowers were placed at the front for immediate use.
- **Six Sigma for Waste Reduction**: Inventory checks were implemented to monitor flower lifespan and minimise waste.

After Implementation:

- **Reduced Flower Waste**: Waste was reduced by 20%, lowering costs.
- **Efficient Workflow**: Organised supplies improved order fulfilment times.
- **Enhanced Customer Satisfaction**: Orders were fulfilled promptly, resulting in happier clients.

Define, Measure, Analyse, Improve, Control

Example 16: Bakery – Organising Ingredients and Standardising Recipes

Sector: Food Services (Bakery)

Background: A bakery had inconsistent product quality and disorganised storage, leading to delays and customer complaints.

Before Implementation:

- **Inconsistent Quality**: Variation in recipe measurements led to inconsistent product quality.
- **Disorganised Ingredients**: Ingredients were scattered, causing delays in preparation.
- **Customer Complaints**: Customers noticed inconsistencies in product quality.

During Implementation:

- **5S for Ingredient Organisation**: Ingredients were stored in labelled containers with designated places, ensuring quick access.
- **Six Sigma Recipe Standardisation**: Standard recipes and portion sizes were implemented to ensure product consistency.

After Implementation:

- **Consistent Product Quality**: Standardised recipes reduced variation, resulting in consistent quality.
- **Faster Preparation**: Organised ingredients reduced prep time by 20%.
- **Increased Customer Satisfaction**: Customers appreciated the consistent quality, leading to more repeat visits.

Define, Measure, Analyse, Improve, Control

Example 17: Dog Grooming Salon – Organising Tools and Reducing Service Times

Sector: Pet Services

Background: A dog grooming salon had long service times and disorganised tools, impacting service quality and client satisfaction.

Before Implementation:

- **Disorganised Tools**: Grooming tools were scattered, causing delays.
- **Long Service Times**: Service times exceeded the client's expectations due to disorganisation.
- **Client Dissatisfaction**: Clients were frustrated with long waits.

During Implementation:

- **5S Tool Organisation**: Tools were organised by type and usage frequency, ensuring groomers had quick access to necessary items.
- **DMAIC for Workflow Optimisation**: The grooming process was standardised to reduce unnecessary steps and improve service flow.

After Implementation:

- **Reduced Service Times**: Grooming times decreased by 30%, allowing for more appointments.
- **Organised Setup**: The organised environment improved groomer efficiency.
- **Higher Client Satisfaction**: Clients appreciated the quicker service, leading to positive reviews.

Define, Measure, Analyse, Improve, Control

Example 18: Professional Photographer – Organising Equipment and Streamlining Editing Workflow

Sector: Creative Services

Background: A photographer struggled with disorganised equipment and a slow photo-editing process, which affected client delivery times.

Before Implementation:

- **Disorganised Equipment**: Cables, lenses, and memory cards were scattered, causing setup delays.
- **Slow Editing Workflow**: The lack of a structured editing process led to extended delivery times.
- **Client Dissatisfaction**: Clients often had to wait longer than expected for their photos.

During Implementation:

- **5S for Equipment Organisation**: Equipment was organised into labelled containers for easy access. Frequently used items were stored in a mobile kit for on-location shoots.
- **Six Sigma Process Standardisation**: The photographer created a standard workflow for editing, including batch processing and present application to speed up editing.
- **Backup and Version Control**: A backup system for photos was implemented, reducing the risk of lost work.

After Implementation:

- **Faster Setup and Editing**: The organised setup and structured editing process reduced turnaround time by 40%.

Define, Measure, Analyse, Improve, Control

- **Efficient Equipment Use**: Quick access to equipment enabled the photographer to work more efficiently on location.
- **Higher Client Satisfaction**: Faster delivery times improved client satisfaction and referrals

Example 19: App Development Start-up, Reducing Bugs and Streamlining Coding Process

Sector: Technology

Background: An app development start-up struggled with high bug rates and disorganised code repositories, leading to longer development times and project delays.

Before Implementation:

- **Frequent Bugs**: The high number of bugs required frequent debugging, delaying project completion.
- **Disorganised Repositories**: Code was not well-organised, making collaboration difficult.
- **Project Delays**: Frequent rework due to bugs pushed back release dates.

During Implementation:

- **5S for Code Organisation**: Code repositories were standardised, with a consistent file-naming system and folder structure. Version control was improved to track code changes.
- **Six Sigma for Bug Reduction**: The DMAIC process was applied to analyse and eliminate common bug sources. The team created a standard checklist for quality checks before code submission.
- **Testing and Standardisation**: Automated testing was introduced to catch bugs early in development.

After Implementation:

- **Reduced Bug Frequency**: Bug occurrence decreased by 35%, reducing time spent on debugging.

Define, Measure, Analyse, Improve, Control

- **Organised Code Repositories**: The organised code structure allowed developers to work collaboratively with fewer issues.
- **Faster Project Completion**: Improved efficiency led to quicker project completion and on-time releases.

Example 20: Boutique Hotel – Reducing Check-in Times and Organising Housekeeping Supplies

Sector: Hospitality

Background: A small boutique hotel faced delays in check-in times, affecting customer satisfaction. Additionally, housekeeping supplies were disorganised, leading to delays in room turnover.

Before Implementation:

- **Long Check-in Times**: Due to inefficient procedures, the check-in process took up to 15 minutes per guest.
- **Disorganised Housekeeping Supplies**: Housekeeping staff spent time searching for supplies, extending room turnover times.
- **Customer Complaints**: Guests were frustrated with the long wait to check in and with delays in room availability.

During Implementation:

- **5S Organisation of Supplies**: The hotel used 5S to organise cleaning supplies and toiletries in a central storage area. Each item was labelled, and high-use items were easily accessible.
- **Six Sigma Standardisation (DMAIC)**: The check-in process was mapped and optimised, with standardised procedures for each step, such as ID verification, payment, and key issuance.
- **Employee Training**: Staff were trained in the new check-in process, and a checklist was implemented to ensure a consistent approach.

After Implementation:

Define, Measure, Analyse, Improve, Control

- **Reduced Check-in Times**: Check-in times were reduced by 40%, leading to shorter waits for guests.
- **Improved Room Turnover**: Organised housekeeping supplies reduced room preparation time by 25%, increasing room availability.
- **Higher Customer Satisfaction**: Guests were pleased with the streamlined check-in and timely room availability, boosting the hotel's ratings.

Define, Measure, Analyse, Improve, Control

Example 21: Real Estate Agency – Streamlining Application Processing and Improving Document Management

Sector: **Real Estate**

Background: A small real estate agency struggled with long tenant application processing times and disorganised document management, leading to client frustration and inefficiencies.

Before Implementation:

- **Delays in Processing Applications**: Tenant applications often took over a week to process due to incomplete information, redundant steps, and disorganised files.
- **Document Clutter**: Paper-based applications and agreements were scattered across desks, making it difficult for agents to retrieve documents when needed.
- **Client Complaints**: The agency frequently received complaints from tenants and property owners about delays and lost documents.

During Implementation:

- **5S Organisation**: The team implemented 5S in their office, creating a central filing system with colour-coded folders for active applications, completed agreements, and archived records. Desks were kept clutter-free, and digital copies of important documents were created.
- **Six Sigma DMAIC Process Analysis**: Using DMAIC, the agency analysed the application process and found redundant steps that slowed processing. They standardised the application review process, implementing a checklist to ensure applications were complete before submission.

Define, Measure, Analyse, Improve, Control

- **Digital Transformation**: The agency introduced digital forms to replace paper applications, reducing data entry time and the risk of lost documents.

After Implementation:

- **Reduced Application Processing Time**: The agency reduced processing time from over a week to 2–3 days by removing redundancies and using a checklist to ensure accuracy.
- **Organised Document Management**: The central filing system and digital copies improved retrieval times by 40%, allowing agents to access client files more quickly.
- **Higher Client Satisfaction**: With a more efficient process, client satisfaction increased as tenants and property owners received faster responses and better service.

www.ingramcontent.com/pod-product-compliance
Lightning Source LLC
Chambersburg PA
CBHW071517220526
45472CB00003B/1052